GO FACTS FOOD

Healthy Eating

Healthy Eating

contents

© Blake Publishing 2003
Additional material © A & C Black Publishers Ltd 2005

First published 2003 in Australia by Blake Education Pty Ltd.

This edition published in the United Kingdom in 2005 by
A & C Black Publishers Ltd, 38 Soho Square, London, W1D 3HB.
www.acblack.com
Reprinted 2007

ISBN 978-0-7136-7289-3

A CIP record for this book is available from the British Library.

Written by Paul McEvoy
Design and layout by The Modern Art Production Group
Photos by Photodisc, Brand X, Corbis, Banana Stock, Stockbyte, Photo Alto, Comstock,
Image DJ, Ingram Publishing, Eyewire and Artvillle.

UK series consultant: Julie Garnett

Printed in China by WKT Company Ltd.

This book is produced using paper that is made from wood grown in managed sustainable
forests. It is natural, renewable and recyclable. The logging and manufacturing processes
conform to the environmental regulations of the country of origin.

4	Healthy Foods
6	Fruit
8	Vegetables
10	Grains
12	Protein
14	Dairy Foods
16	Sugars, Fats and Oils
18	Table, Glossary and Index

Healthy Foods

Your body needs a variety of good foods to grow and stay healthy.

The food we eat is called our **diet**. A balanced diet contains a wide variety of foods.

Carbohydrates in foods such as bread and rice give us energy. Other foods, like fruits and vegetables, are full of vitamins and minerals.

We need protein to make muscles, skin and hair. Meat and eggs are high-protein foods. We need calcium for our teeth and bones. Dairy foods, like cheese and milk, are high in calcium.

Bowl of rice

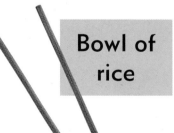

Fresh fruit and vegetables

This meal contains carbohydrates, vitamins and minerals.

Vegetables can be mixed with many different foods such as pasta.

Meat and seafood are high-protein foods.

Fruit

Fruits have many vitamins and minerals that our bodies need.

Fruits contain vitamins, minerals and natural sugars. This means they taste good and are good for you. Fruits also contain **fibre**, which helps **digestion**.

Citrus fruits, such as oranges and lemons, are high in vitamin C. Vitamin C helps build strong **joints**, healthy skin and helps us fight illness.

Fresh fruit

6

Most fruits are more than 90 percent water.

Grains, fruits and vegetables are good sources of fibre.

Freshly squeezed fruit juice is full of vitamins and flavour.

7

Vegetables

Eating plenty of vegetables helps you get all the vitamins and minerals you need.

We can eat vegetables raw, or cooked, or drink them as juice. Celery and carrots can be eaten raw. Peas and beans are sweet when they're cooked. Tomatoes and carrots make delicious juices.

Carrots and sweet potatoes contain vitamin A. We need vitamin A for good eyesight and to fight **infections**.

Vegetables also contain calcium and iron. These minerals help keep our bones strong and make new red blood cells.

Fresh vegetables

8

Fresh fruits and vegetables are the healthiest for our bodies.

Tomatoes, broccoli and red peppers are high in vitamin C.

GO FACT!

FIRST!
The first frozen vegetable ever sold was spinach.

Markets sell a wide variety of fresh vegetables.

9

Grains

A healthy diet should include plenty of grains, such as wheat, rice and corn.

Some grain is cooked and eaten whole. Other grain is ground into flour to make bread, pasta and cereals. Grains have carbohydrates which give the body energy.

Wholegrain foods are a good way to eat carbohydrates. Some wholegrain foods are corn on the cob, rice, and wholegrain bread. They are high in fibre. Whole grains contain magnesium, a mineral that helps build strong bones and teeth.

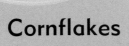

Cornflakes

Bread rolls

Breakfast cereal gives us energy for the day ahead.

Rice can be boiled or cooked with other ingredients.

Wholegrain foods are healthiest for our bodies.

Sandwiches can be made with white, brown or wholegrain bread.

11

Protein

Meat, fish, milk and eggs are all high in protein.

Protein is important for building muscles. Many people get their protein from meat, eggs, fish or other seafood. These high-protein foods also contain iron, vitamins and minerals. One of these vitamins is B_{12}. Our bodies need B_{12} to make new red blood cells.

Some people are vegetarians. This means they eat no meat. Vegetarians can get protein from plants such as peas, nuts and soyabeans.

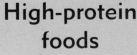

High-protein foods

Soya products

Soyabeans are the most nutritious beans.

The protein in fish is easily absorbed by our bodies.

Meats are usually cooked to kill any bacteria that can make people sick.

GO FACT!

MOST!
Fish is the biggest source of protein for the people of the world.

13

Dairy Foods

Dairy foods are an important source of calcium for growing bodies.

Dairy foods are usually made from cows' milk. Milk is made into cheese, yoghurt, butter and ice-cream. Dairy foods are high in calcium. Calcium builds strong bones and teeth.

Some people are **allergic** to cows' milk. They can drink milk made from soyabeans or rice. Vitamins and calcium are added to soya and rice milk to make them as nutritious as cows' milk.

Calcium-rich foods

Vitamins A and D are often added to milk.

There are many types of cheese.

Buffalo milk can be used to make mozzarella cheese.

Yoghurt provides us with calcium and protein and helps digestion.

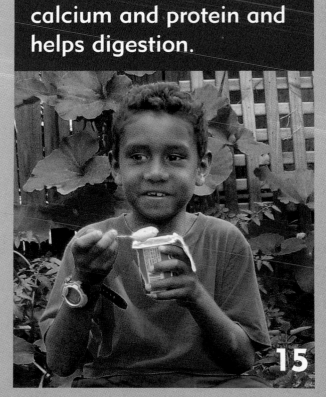

15

Sugars, Fats and Oils

A healthy diet has only small amounts of sugars, fats and oils. They provide energy but are low in other things our bodies need.

Olive oil

Sugar is a high-energy food but it doesn't contain any vitamins, minerals or protein. Foods such as lollies, ice-cream and fizzy drinks are high in sugar. Eating too much sugar can cause tooth **decay**.

We need some fats and oils to help our bodies **absorb** some vitamins. We also use some fats to grow new **nerves**. The body stores any fat that isn't used. Without plenty of exercise, eating a lot of sugar and fat can make us overweight.

Fried chicken

16

Oils made from vegetables, nuts and seeds are often used in salad dressing.

Sweets are high in sugar but low in the other things our bodies need.

We often eat foods high in sugar at parties.

GO FACT!

DID YOU KNOW?
Peanut oil is used for cooking in submarines because it doesn't smoke unless heated above 232°C.

What Foods Contain?

Carbohydrates

Protein
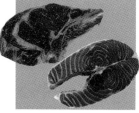   

Fibre

Fats and Oils

Sugars

Glossary

absorb	take in
allergic	reacting badly to something
citrus	fruits such as oranges and lemons
decay	to rot and cause cavities
diet	the food we eat every day
digestion	the process of breaking down food so our bodies can use it
fibre	a part of food that helps digestion
infection	disease caused by germs
joint	where your body bends, such as a knee, ankle, elbow or hip
nerve	part of the body that carries messages to and from the brain and the sense organs

Index

bread 4, 10

calcium 4, 8, 14

carbohydrates 4, 10

dairy foods 4, 14

diet 4, 16

energy 4, 16

fat 16

fibre 6, 10

fish 12

fruit 4, 6

grains 10

iron 8

lollies 16

meat 4, 12

milk 4, 14

minerals 4, 6, 8, 10, 12, 16

pasta 10

protein 4, 12

rice 4, 10, 14

seafood 12

soyabeans 12, 14

vegetarian 12

vitamins 4, 6, 8, 12, 14, 16